Forest Wildflowers

Showy Wildflowers of the Woods, Mountains and Forests of the Northern Rocky Mountain States

photography and text by
Dee Strickler

illustration and graphic design by
Zoe Strickler

Front Cover: Orchid Family *(Orchidaceae)*

FAIRYSLIPPER, Calypso
Calypso bulbosa (L.) Oakes. Among the flowers of the world, the orchids must surely rank as the most enchanting. Not all of our orchids have spectacular blossoms, but Fairyslipper does. The overall color varies from pale pink to deep magenta. One inflated petal forms the slipper, tipped with two horn-like projections below the toe. Exquisite purple stripes decorate the slipper inside and below and bright yellow hairs and purple spots adorn the top. Two other petals and three sepals, all narrow and sharp pointed, effect a starry purple crown. Each plant has a single stem, 2 to 6 inches high, two or three clasping bracts on the stem and one broadly oval leaf that emerges in the fall and overwinters under the snow. It blooms early in the season, soon after snow melt. HABITAT: Moist woods with a layer of duff, from the sea coast to medium elevations in the mountains. RANGE: Transcontinental in Canada and Alaska, south to northeastern U.S., New Mexico and N California. COMMENT: Calypso Orchid can be locally abundant, but logging has destroyed vast areas of its habitat. All orchids should be considered rare or endangered and should never be picked or transplanted.

Library of Congress Catalog Card Number: 88-80229
ISBN 1-931832-34-x

Published by The Flower Press
Columbia Falls, Montana

Publishing Consultant
Riverbend Publishing
Helena, Montana

To order extra copies of this book contact:
The Flower Press, 192 Larch Lane, Columbia Falls, MT 59912

Riverbend Publishing, P.O. Box 5833, Helena, MT 59604, toll free
1-866-787-2363, www.riverbendpublishing.com.

Printed in South Korea.

Sixth Printing, revised 2003

Acknowledgements

The author owes a debt of gratitude to numerous people for help in plant identification, proofreading and other assistance in the preparation of this book. Special thanks and appreciation are extended to Dr. Jeanette Oliver, botanist at Flathead Valley Community College, Kalispell, Montana and to Peter Lesica, rare plant specialist, Missoula, Montana and Peter Stickney, USDA Forest Service, Missoula for help in identifying difficult species. Many of the flowers pictured have been pressed, dried and deposited in the herbarium of FVCC.

I wish also to recognize the kind assistance of Drs. Adolph Hecht, Amy Gilmartin and Joy Mastroguiseppe of Washington State University and Dr. Kathleen Peterson and Jeffrey Strachan of the University of Montana.

My daughter Zoe Strickler contributed substantially with constructive criticism and the graphic design and art work.

Finally, I thank my wife, Claire, for patient help in picture selection, for help with the manuscript and for constant support and encouragement.

—Whitefish, Montana, Revised March 2003

About the author

Dee Strickler is a Wood Scientist and Technologist holding a B.S. from Washington State University, M,S. from Syracuse University and a doctorate from Duke University. His forestry undergraduate curriculum included a minor in botany. As Wood Technologist on the College of Engineering Faculty of Washington State University for many years, he authored over 50 technical publications and reports on original research in the fields of wood properties and glued wood products.

Dr. Strickler has enjoyed wildflower photography for more than 20 years and herein shares that interest and enjoyment with others.

Contents

Introduction

Forest Wildflowers is the second of a three volume series on the showy flowering plants of the northern Rocky Mountain states. The first volume, *Prairie Wildflowers,* 1986, introduced the wildflowers of the plains, valleys, deserts and foothills of the region and volume III, *Alpine Wildflowers*, will complete the series.

These guide books help hikers, outdoorsmen, travelers, amateur botanists and all lovers of nature who want to know "What flower is that?" Professional botanists and range managers find them a useful supplement to more authoritative works on the flora of the northern Rockies. School teachers and students from elementary schools to universities also may use them as beginner's guides to botany and wildflower appreciation.

The flowers in this book appear in family sequence. The system of grouping flowers by color is not used, because wide color variations frequently occur within a single species and color is not a reliable indicator for species identification.

For each flower pictured, some of the most noticeable features are described, including the leaves, blooming period, habitat and range in which the plant grows. Some pertinent comments of general interest about the species or family usually conclude the discussion.

The flowers shown in this or any similar guide can only include a sample of the seemingly endless array in our natural world. The comments in the text frequently mention other closely related species that one may encounter. A beautiful wildflower to one person may represent a noxious weed to another. The author hopes that a fair balance has been achieved and that everyone can find beauty and pleasure among these pages.

The specific region where wildflowers were photographed for this book include Idaho, Montana, Wyoming, northern Utah and Colorado and eastern Oregon and Washington. The ranges of many of the flowers pictured, however, extend over much wider areas.

Montane Forests

The Rocky Mountains form the backbone of our continent and large variations in altitude commonly occur. Elevations range from about 1,000 feet in the river bottoms that empty into the Columbia River on the northwestern edge of our region to more than 14,000 feet atop numerous Colorado peaks. Generally montane or mountain forests, where the flowers shown in this book can be found, cover an intermediate life zone between the open, treeless prairies and the alpine heights above timberline.

Our national forests incorporate the major portion of forests and woodlands in the northern Rockies. Additional forests are included in many state lands and state and national parks, monuments and wildlife refuges. The federal Bureau of Land Management also controls significant forest acreage. Wildflower enthusiasts may freely explore most of these government lands and one can obtain maps for a nominal fee from the appropriate government offices. Timber companies and other private interests own considerable forest acreage also, but one should obtain permission to enter private lands.

Precipitation that nurtures forest growth falls more heavily on the higher elevations of the region than on the surrounding lowlands. The forests in the north commonly receive more moisture than those in the southerly portion. Westerly slopes are generally wetter than easterly slopes, because the weather pattern prevails from west to east. North facing slopes, moreover, support more forest cover, because they do not receive direct drying rays from the sun.

Forests normally develop soils rich in humus in the upper layers including a layer of duff or non-decomposed organic material on top. Some flowering plants thrive only under a forest canopy, such as members of the Orchid and Heath families, several of which are parasites or saprophytes. Other species require the stronger sunlight of forest openings or fringes. Those flowering plants that require concentrated sunlight do not grow in dense forests.

Many of our forests have been profoundly altered by logging and road building. When the forest cover is removed and the soil disturbed, some species cannot survive and may not return when the forest regenerates. Still other species flourish on disturbed sites, including some introduced from other parts of the country or the world.

Within the montane forest zone several distinct types of forest occur and the flowering plants associated with them vary accordingly. The various forest types may also intermix with each other. As one travels from the dry open prairie upward into the mountains, one may encounter a transitional woodland-shrub belt. This is commonly pinon-juniper, found in the southern part of the region and east of the continental divide. On the north and westerly sides, other shrubs such as mountain mahogany, ninebark and black hawthorn signal the transition. Flowering shrubs provide some of our prettiest wildflowers.

Ponderosa pine generally predominates in the lower elevation forests and on the drier sites. Typically the trees are scattered in parklike openings and meadows. Many prairie wildflowers invade these open stands. Higher up the slopes forests are dominated by Douglas fir. Heavier rainfall makes these stands more dense. Douglas fir may also intermix with other tree species, commonly ponderosa pine and larch.

On still wetter sites true firs and spruces displace Douglas fir. These forests occupy the higher elevations, the canyon bottoms and the north slopes. Here too, one may find aspen or lodgepole pine. These latter two species often occur as more or less pure stands and tend to develop soon after and as a result of wild fire.

In the southern Rockies montane forests begin around 8,000 feet elevation or even higher on south facing slopes. In the north, forests commonly begin at about 5,000 feet east of the continental divide, but at 2,500 feet on the moister west slopes or even lower in the valleys and canyon bottoms.

In the protected valleys and canyons of the northwestern portion of the region grow forests containing western redcedar and hemlock.

These remnants of wet coastal forests of the Pacific Northwest harbor flowering herbs and shrubs common to wet coastal forest, such as skunk cabbage and devil's club.

Above the montane forests one finds a transitional subalpine forest zone. Here subalpine fir, spruce and the five-needle pines flourish. These trees are generally stunted on exposed sites. Flowering plants of this subalpine zone intergrade more commonly into the alpine flora above timberline than into the montane forests. Many subalpine flowers will therefore appear in Vol. III, *Alpine Wildflowers*.

Naming of Plants

Botanists worldwide have developed a system of nomenclature that will accommodate any plant. Within this system each flowering, seed-producing plant belongs to a family, genus and species. Families are groups with broad similarities. Each family contains several or many genera (plural of genus) and within each genus there are many unique species. Further classification may also differentiate varieties within a species.

Scientific names have Latin endings and are therefore italicized in print. The family name is usually dropped because the genus–species binomial sufficiently defines a specific plant. For example, the name *Iris missouriensis* gives the genus first and then the species. The scientific binomial carries an appendage giving the name of the authority(ies) the author recognizes as having originated the proper names.

Most wildflowers also have one or more common names that have come about through general usage. In the interest of space, not all of the common names are given for flowers that have many such names.

Map of Northern Rocky Mountains where flowers in this book occur

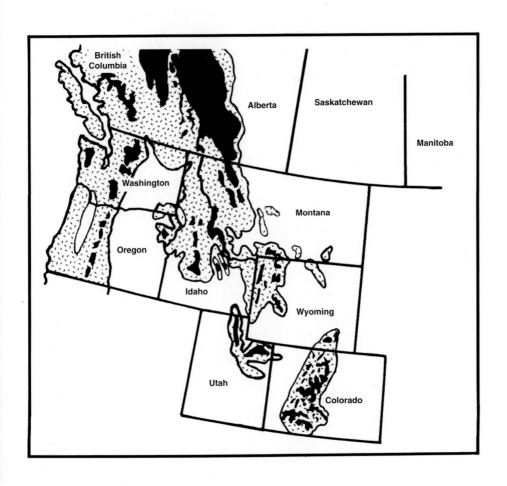

British Columbia

Alberta

Saskatchewan

Manitoba

Washington

Montana

Oregon

Idaho

Wyoming

Utah

Colorado

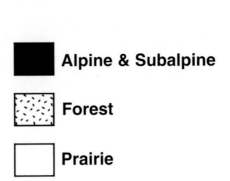

■ Alpine & Subalpine

▦ Forest

□ Prairie

Arum or Calla Lily Family *(Araceae)*

YELLOW SKUNK CABBAGE

Lysichitum americanum H. & S. These flowers, among the earliest in the spring, emerge before their leaves do, on an unbranched fleshy stalk or spike, 6 to 12 inches tall. A multitude of tiny blossoms cover the stalk. A yellow hood-like bract, called a spathe, partly encloses the inflorescence. The leaves of this perennial mature later and are generally 2 to 3 feet long and 1 foot wide, the largest of any native plant.

HABITAT: Skunk Cabbage inhabits wet woods, stream banks and bogs at elevations up to 4,000 feet. RANGE: W Montana and N Idaho, west to the Pacific Coast, Alaska to California. COMMENT: Wild animals, especially bears, feed on skunk cabbage in the spring. All parts of the plant are edible, but should be boiled to reduce the concentration of oxalic acid which produces a bitter taste.

Lily Family *(Liliaceae)*

Lily Family *(Liliaceae)*

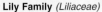

SHORT STYLED ONION

Allium brevistylum Wats. This wild onion has relatively few blossoms arranged in a tight umbel. Two papery bracts, that are united at the base, subtend the umbel. Individual flowers, about ¼ inch long, vary from pink to rose. Two or more grass-like leaves grow from the base shorter than the 10 to 20 inch stem, which flattens toward the top. A grayish brown membrane covers the slender bulb. Look for these choice wildflowers in the summer. HABITAT: Wet places from lower montane to subalpine. RANGE: N Utah and Colorado to Idaho and Montana.

NODDING ONION

Allium cernuum Roth. A distinctive wild onion that nods gracefully to forest visitors. It has white to pink petals, rounded at the tip. The stamens protrude beyond the petals. Each individual flower hangs from a slender pedicel, giving the inflorescence an exquisite starburst effect. The long, slender bulbs grow in clusters. Blooms in early summer. HABITAT: Moist but usually well drained soils from low to high elevations. RANGE: Most mountainous regions of North America from Mexico to Canada, except California and the Blue Mountains of E Oregon and Washington and adjacent W Idaho.

Lily Family *(Liliaceae)*

POINTED (BAKER'S) MARIPOSA LILY

Calochortus apiculatus Baker. Stunning white flowers, 2 to 3 inches across, with three broadly oval petals and three narrow sepals. The inner face of a petal has several long hairs and a small oval or nearly round purple gland near the base. Close examination reveals a sharp point on the end of each stamen. A smooth upright stem, 6 to 12 inches tall, supports one to five flowers and carries two or three leafy bracts near the top. A single basal leaf grows somewhat shorter than the floral stem, about ¼ inch wide and flat, tapering to a point. Flowers bloom in early summer. HABITAT: Coniferous woods and forest openings. RANGE: Southern Canada on both sides of the Rockies to Montana and Idaho. COMMENT: Mariposa means "butterfly" in Spanish.

Lily Family *(Liliaceae)*

HAIRY CAT'S EAR, Elegant Mariposa

Calochortus elegans Pursh. This densely hairy mariposa grows lower and smaller than any other species in our region. One to seven flowers per plant display a greenish white tinge outside and a purple cast on the hairs within. Stylish purple crescents decorate the inner faces of the petals and sepals. Each plant has just one long leaf that overtops the flowers. Look for it in late spring. HABITAT: Coniferous woods and forest margins from medium to high elevation. RANGE: Montana to California.

Lily Family *(Liliaceae)*

BIG POD MARIPOSA TULIP

Calochortus eurycarpus Wats. Near the base of each petal this gorgeous mariposa lily has a bright yellow oval or triangular gland, fringed with a purplish membrane and a few scattered hairs. A broad green vertical stripe above the gland leads to a dark purple accent that may be oval or narrow and gracefully arched. The broad petals are rounded or have a slight point at the tip. One narrow, channeled leaf clasps the stem. Blooms from early to mid summer. HABITAT: Open slopes and scattered timber to high montane. RANGE: W Montana and Wyoming to SE Washington and N Nevada.

Lily Family *(Liliaceae)*

GREEN BANDED STAR TULIP

Calochortus macrocarpus Dougl. This glorious mariposa lily has three sharp narrow sepals that are generally longer than the petals. A narrow, longitudinal green stripe decorates the middle of each petal, noticeable on the back if not on the face. The flowers appear from late spring to summer depending on elevation. HABITAT: Dry open prairie to moderately high elevations in the mountains. RANGE: Central Washington to W Montana and south to Nevada and NE California.

Lily Family *(Liliaceae)*

Lily Family *(Liliaceae)*

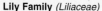

QUEEN'S CUP, Bride's Bonnet, Bead Lily

Clintonia unitflora (Schult.) Kunth.
A stylish white lily with three petals and three sepals all uniform in size. The solitary flower terminates a peduncle about 4 inches high, naked except for a small linear bract near the top. Two or three bright green, broadly oval and parallel veined leaves compose a perfect setting for the blossom on the forest floor. Queen's Cup blooms in early summer and a round, blue berry develops in late summer. HABITAT: Deep forests at low to mid elevations. RANGE: Alaska to California and east to Montana.

WARTBERRY FAIRYBELL

Disporum trachycarpum (Wats.) Britt.
This 1 to 2 foot tall leafy perennial branches once or twice. Pairs of cream colored floral bells, about ½ inch long droop from the ends of the branches. One may overlook them, because the oval, parallel veined leaves often hide the flowers. Many wart-like projections cover the berries, which change color as they ripen from green to yellow to orange or deep red. They commonly bloom in May and June. HABITAT: Moist woods. RANGE: Canadian Rockies south to Colorado, Nebraska, and Arizona. COMMENT: Two species of fairybell inhabit the Rockies. Hooker's Fairybell occurs in the northern portion of the range of Wartberry Fairybell.

Lily Family *(Liliaceae)*

GLACIER LILY, Dogtooth Violet

Erythronium grandiflorum Pursh. Six tepals (petals and sepals) spread widely or reflex backward. They are brilliant yellow or cream colored, lance-shaped and 1 to 1½ inches long. Two broad oval leaves, smooth and bright green, grow from the base. The plants grow 6 to 10 inches tall from an elongated bulb or corm. Six conspicuous anthers may vary from white to yellow, red or purple. The blooms emerge soon after snowmelt, depending on elevation, from March to August. HABITAT: Nearly ubiquitous from low open sites to forests to high alpine ridges and meadows. RANGE: SW Canada and NW U.S., south to Colorado. COMMENT: Of the four species of *Erythronium* in the Northwest, we have only one in the Rockies, but we have three varieties of Glacier Lily. The cream variety shown, var. *candidum,* occurs in shady forests in E Washington, N Idaho and W Montana. The yellow varieties which thrive from low prairies to high alpine are represented in Vol. III, *Alpine Wildflowers.*

Glacier Lily has many common names such as dogtooth violet, trout lily, fawn lily and adder's tongue. All parts of the plant are edible and bears frequently feed on them in the spring. A near relative is the famous avalanche lily of the Cascades and Olympics.

Lily Family *(Liliaceae)*

COLUMBIA LILY, Tiger Lily
Lilium columbianum Hanson.
A stunning classical lily with six orange spotted tepals, strongly recurved backward. The plants stand 2 to 4 feet tall. The smooth elliptical leaves may appear whorled or scattered on the stalk. Look for this gorgeous wildflower in late spring or early summer.
HABITAT: Coniferous woods and forest margins. RANGE: B.C. to California in the Cascades and east to NW Montana. COMMENT: Wood lily, *L. philadelphicum,* the floral emblem of Saskatchewan, does not have the strongly reflexed petals. It grows along the Rocky Mountain front and eastward. Both species are considered rare and endangered and should never be disturbed.

Lily Family *(Liliaceae)*

FALSE SOLOMON'S SEAL
Smilacina racemosa L.
A distinctive mass of tiny white blossoms on many short branching stems form a panicle. The large, broadly oval leaves have parallel veins and clasp the stem, which may grow to 3 feet tall. In summer the fruit develop a reddish to orange berry, usually quite wrinkled. Look for them in the spring. HABITAT: Coniferous woods and stream banks. RANGE: North America, south to California and Georgia.

STAR FLOWERED SOLOMON PLUME
Smilacina Stellata (L.) Desf.
This species grows smaller than False Solomon's Seal, with narrower leaves. Individually the flowers are larger, but much less numerous, even few in number. The berry, about ½ inch in diameter, is green at first and then turns yellow or dark brown. It blooms in mid to late spring. HABITAT: Woods, both moist and well drained. RANGE: Transcontinental, south in the Rockies to Arizona. Both species are common forest inhabitants.

Lily Family *(Liliaceae)*

Lily Family *(Liliaceae)*

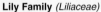

TWISTED STALK

Streptopus amplexifolius (L.) DC. A smooth leafy plant, 1½ to 3 feet tall, with broadly lance-shaped leaves, 3 or 4 inches long, clasping the stems. Several branches originate in the leaf axils. Small bell-shaped, cream-colored flowers hang pendent along the stem on rather long pedicels, which have distinct kinks at midlength. The fruit are smooth oval berries, normally red or sometimes yellow. One may easily overlook the flowers or berries concealed beneath the leaves. Blooms in May and June. HABITAT: Look for Twisted Stalk on wet stream banks in woods and thickets. RANGE: Most of North America, north of Mexico.

FALSE HELLEBORE

Veratrum californicum Durand. Stout unbranched stalks stand 4 to 6 feet tall with numerous parallel veined leaves, 8 to 10 inches long, clasping the stems. The flowers create an elongated mass of small white blossoms on short lateral branches as well as the tip of the main stem. False Hellebore blooms in summer. HABITAT: Wet places in woods and meadows from low to high elevation. RANGE: N Idaho to SW Montana and south to Mexico and west to the Pacific Coast. COMMENT: Indian Hellebore, *V. viride,* a close relative, has green flowers and inhabits higher elevations in the northern portion of our region.

Orchid Family *(Orchidaceae)*

SPOTTED CORALROOT

Corallorhiza maculata Raf. The coralroots possess no green leaves and are variously classed as saprophytes or parasites. Saprophytes rely on decayed organic material for sustenance. Technically, coralroots are parasites on specific fungi that decay organic matter in the forest floor. These fascinating orchids send up numerous stems, 8 to 18 inches tall, from spreading underground rhizomes. Several bracts clasp the yellow to purple or brownish stems. An open, spike-like raceme of 10 to 30 flowers occupies the upper $1/2$ to $1/3$ of the stem. A yellow tubular ovary forms the basal half of the flower. Three reddish to purple sepals and two upper petals arch gracefully over and around the lower lip formed by the third petal. Wine red or purple spots embellish the lip, which is white or pale pink. The two upper petals may also be spotted, but less noticeably. Albino specimens occur frequently and may easily be mistaken for Yellow Coralroot, *C. trifida.* Blooms from May to August. HABITAT: Woods and forests. RANGE: Transcontinental in the U.S. and S Canada.

19

Orchid Family *(Orchidaceae)*

Orchid Family *(Orchidaceae)*

MERTEN'S CORALROOT, Western Coralroot

Corallorhiza mertensiana Bong. Differs from Spotted Coralroot in the flowers, which open widely about $^1/_2$ to $^3/_4$ inch long. The delicate red to pink lip hangs pendent, recurves outward and has two small teeth on the sides. Two sepals and the lip petal fuse at the base to form a small sac or spur under the lip. Look for these captivating beauties in mid summer. HABITAT: Deep coniferous forest. RANGE: Wyoming, Idaho and N California, north to Alaska.

STRIPED CORALROOT

Corallorhiza striata Lindl. Striped Coralroot stands 6 to 16 inches tall, has several clasping bracts on purplish stems and a spike-like raceme of up to 30 flowers on the upper half of the stem. A lower petal, an enlarged lip, is deep maroon to purple and concave with thickened margins. Two other petals and three sepals, usually pinkish with three red to purple stripes, droop gracefully over the lip, blooming from mid spring to early summer. HABITAT: Deep moist woods. RANGE. Across Canada and south in the western mountains to Mexico. COMMENT: Never very abundant.

Orchid Family *(Orchidaceae)*

YELLOW LADY'S SLIPPER

Cypripedium calceolus L. This breathtaking orchid, quite similar to Mountain Lady's Slipper in general form, has narrower leaves and usually only one flower on each stem. The lip petal or slipper is intense yellow and about 1 inch long, the upper sepal and petals pale yellow or purple and twisted. It blooms in late May and June. HABITAT: Moist woods or marshy areas. RANGE: Circumpolar; across S Canada and south to Oregon, Utah, Colorado, Minnesota and New York. COMMENT: Yellow Lady's Slipper is extremely rare in our part of the Rockies and should never be picked or transplanted. It may now be extinct in Oregon.

Orchid Family *(Orchidaceae)*

MOUNTAIN LADY'S SLIPPER

Cypripedium montanum Dougl. The queen of Rocky Mountain orchids! The lower petal inflates broadly into a lustrous white pouch or slipper, about 1 inch long, prominently ribbed, sometimes with purplish veins. One sepal and two petals have brownish or purplish stripes and twist gracefully over the slipper. They are about 2 inches long. Two other sepals below the slipper unite into one for most of their length. A brilliant yellow "column," usually spotted red or purple, accents the throat of the slipper. Fused stamens and pistils form the column, a feature that identifies all orchids. The plant stands 1 to 2 feet tall, has one to three blossoms and numerous broadly oval, luxuriant, parallel-veined leaves. The leaves clasp the stem and blossoms emerge from axils of the upper leaves. Look for this breathtaking beauty mostly in June. It will make your day to find it. HABITAT: Moist but well drained mountain slopes and woods. RANGE: Wyoming to Alberta and N California to Alaska. COMMENT: Three other species of *Cypripedium* inhabit the Rockies. All are rare and possibly endangered.

Orchid Family *(Orchidaceae)*   **Orchid Family** *(Orchidaceae)*

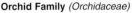

PHANTOM ORCHID

Eburophyton austinae (Gray) Heller. A strange spellbinding ghost on the forest floor. Phantom Orchid is sheer white or ivory color overall, turning brown with age. It lacks green leaves and is therefore a saprophyte, relying on a fungus in its roots to obtain sustenance from decaying organic matter in the soil. The plants stand 8 to 20 inches tall, the leaves reduced to mere clasping bracts. The lower petal forms a small open sac and has a yellowish spot in the throat, the only color on the plant. The petals and sepals, about ³/₄ inch long and narrowly elliptical, shield or cup the short lip and column. Blooms from June to early August. HABITAT: Well drained, medium-dense forest. RANGE: Idaho to the Pacific Coast, Washington to California. COMMENT: *Eburophyton* has only one known species.

ROUND LEAVED REIN ORCHID

Habenaria orbiculata (Pursh) Torr. This rein or bog orchid produces a single unbranched stem 8 to 24 inches tall. Two oval leaves, rather thick and leathery, 3 to 6 inches long and nearly as wide, grow from the base of the plant and lie flat on the ground. From 5 to 25 white, cream or greenish white flowers create a loose raceme at the top of the stem. The upper sepal stands erect and spreads broadly, while two narrower sepals droop on either side. Two small upper petals have thickened, club shaped tips that resemble eyes. Attached in the middle, the front half of the lower petal droops in a long narrow lip and the back half forms a slender curving spur nearly 1 inch long. Overall the frontal effect is that of a funny clown's face. It blooms early in summer. HABITAT: Deep, damp, boreal forest. RANGE: Alaska to Newfoundland and south in the west to Oregon, Idaho and Montana.

Orchid Family *(Orchidaceae)*

WHITE BOG ORCHID

Habenaria dilatata (Pursh) Hook. Stately unbranched stems, ½ to 3 feet tall. Luxurious lance-shaped leaves clasp the stem at the base and grow smaller and sessile upward. A dense spike of white, fragrant orchids, about ½ inch across, clothe the upper stem. The pure white lip droops gracefully in front and curves backward and downward into a slender hollow spur. One sepal and two petals create a hood over the lip and two sepals spread wide on the sides. Blooms in summer. HABITAT: Wet ground or bogs. RANGE: Northern North America, south to New Mexico and

California. COMMENT: All orchids must be pollinated by insects. They never self pollinate. Many species have evolved special shapes and structures to coincide with the size, shape and habits of specific insects. The life cycles of orchids and insects are often interdependent. Orchid pollination presents a fascinating field of study.

In *Habenaria* the spur holds nectar on which insects feed. Only insects with long flexible tongues, usually moths, can reach the nectar. Directly above the opening to the spur sits the column coated with pollen. An insect's forehead comes in contact with the pollen when it sticks its tongue into the spur.

Orchid Family *(Orchidaceae)*

HOODED LADIES' TRESSES

Spiranthes romanzoffiana Cham. This orchid has one to four rows of flowers in a dense spike that twists around the upper stem. Each blossom sprouts from the axil of a leafy bract. Narrow lance-shaped leaves, 3 to 10 inches long, sheath the base of the stem, which may reach 2 feet tall. The cream colored flowers have pendent lower lips, curled on the edges. The other petals and sepals form an upper hood. It differs from bog orchids by the lack of a spur. Look for Ladies' Tresses in mid summer. HABITAT: Moist ground, boggy to well drained, from seashore to subalpine. RANGE: U.S. and Canada except for southeast United States.

Parsley Family *(Apiaceae, Umbelliferae)*

Parsley Family *(Apiaceae, Umbelliferae)*

COW PARSNIP

Heracleum lanatum Michx. Coarse plants, 3 to 9 feet high, with three-bladed pinnate leaves to 1 foot across. The basal leaves spread much wider than the upper ones, the leaflets palmately lobed (maple-like) and sharply toothed on the margins. Leafy wings flank the primary leaf petioles. Large flat topped compound umbels terminate the main stalks and smaller ones originate in upper leaf axils. These plants sometimes form dense patches on choice sites. They bloom in summer. HABITAT: Moist ground or deep, well drained soil from low to subalpine elevations. RANGE: Widespread and common in North America and Asia.

LYALL'S ANGELICA, Sharptooth Angelica

Angelica arguta Nutt. These plants send up single, unbranched stems 2 to 6 feet tall. White compound umbels (twice umbellate) describe the flowers. The large leaves are twice pinnately compound, growing smaller upward. They have long leaf petioles, graced by leafy wings at the base. Petiole wings of the upper leaves appear as simple stem leaves in the picture. Sharp teeth mark the edges of the leaflets. Look for these flowers in the summer. HABITAT: Moist or wet meadows from low to moderate elevations in the mountains. RANGE: Southern Alberta and British Columbia to Utah and N California. COMMENT: Lyall's Angelica is not reported to be poisonous, but several other members of the parsley family can be deadly for humans and livestock.

Dogbane Family *(Apocynaceae)*

Ginseng Family *(Araliaceae)*

SPREADING DOGBANE

Apocynum androsaemifolium (L.)
These pretty little bell-shaped flowers
are about ¼ inch long and white to pink
on the outside to bright pink or red
striped inside. The flowers cluster on
branch ends and originate in the
uppermost leaf axils. The oval leaves,
smooth on the margins and surfaces,
tend to droop. Milky sap characterizes
these plants that stand 1 to 2 feet tall.
They bloom in late spring and early
summer. HABITAT: Fairly deep, well
drained soil in valleys to medium
elevation in the mountains. RANGE:
Most of the U.S. and Canada.
COMMENT: Four poorly defined
species of dogbane inhabit
North America. The flowers of all
appear quite similar. Dogbane can be a
pest to farmers.

DEVIL'S CLUB (berries)

Oplopanax horridum (T. & G.) Miq.
Fierce yellow spines cover the rambling
woody stems that grow 3 to 10 feet
high. Large maple-like leaves, 4 to 12
inches broad, also have spines on the
peduncles and veins. The small
yellowish white flowers are borne in a
dense spiky raceme or panicle. Bright
red berries replace the flowers in mid to
late summer. HABITAT: Deep moist
woods and stream banks, usually
where western redcedar and hemlock
trees provide an understory. RANGE:
W Montana, N Idaho and west to
Oregon and Alaska. Also around the
Great Lakes and northward.

Birthwort Family *(Aristolochiaceae)*

WILD GINGER

Asarum caudatum Lindl. The leaves of this unusual plant are roundly heart-shaped, 2 to 6 inches broad, on hairy stems to 8 inches high. Held horizontally, they create a dense groundcover, commonly hiding the stems and flowers. The fascinating blossoms grow at the base of the plant and display three purple or brown bracts, 2 to 3 inches long, that taper to linear points. It blooms from April to July. HABITAT: Shaded woods, frequently in moist canyon bottoms. RANGE: W Montana to the coast of British Columbia and California.

PEARLY EVERLASTING

Anaphalis margaritacea (L.) B & H. Papery white bracts impart to these rounded clusters of stark white flowers their distinctive appearance. They lack ray florets. The plants stand 1 to 2 feet tall. Woolly white hairs cover the narrow alternate leaves. The plant spreads from extensive underground roots. Blossoms appear in mid to late summer. HABITAT: Typically in forest openings. Pearly Everlasting sometimes covers large clear-cut areas in the mountains soon after logging and provides valuable protection against erosion. RANGE: Much of mountainous North America, especially in the West and in Asia. COMMENT: Makes excellent dried flower arrangements. It can easily be mistaken for several species of pussytoes.

Sunflower Family *(Asteraceae, Compositae)*

Sunflower Family *(Asteraceae, Compositae)*

Sunflower Family *(Asteraceae, Compositae)*

ROSE PUSSYTOES

Antennaria microphylla Rydb. These pretty little pink to red floral heads lack ray florets. Papery bracts that surround the disc flowers carry the red coloration. The plant is mat forming, spreading by stolons which are aerial runners. They take root where they touch the ground. Dense gray hairs cover the stems and small spatula-shaped leaves. Rose Pussytoes bloom from May to August. HABITAT: Open woods and forests to meadows and prairies. RANGE: Alaska and N Canada, south in the mountains to California and New Mexico.

HEARTLEAF ARNICA

Arnica cordifolia Hook. Engaging yellow to nearly orange composites, they produce stems 6 to 20 inches high with two to four pairs of opposite, heart-shaped leaves. Shallow notches scallop the ends of the ray petals. The leaves have irregular teeth on the margins. Heartleaf Arnica spreads from extensive underground roots, does not crowd itself and many shoots bear leaves only. Blooms from April to June. HABITAT: Deep, coniferous, well-drained forests and open woods from low to subalpine elevations. RANGE: The Rocky Mountains from Alaska to New Mexico. COMMMENT: One can find a dozen species of Arnica in the Rockies.

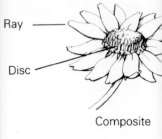

Ray

Disc

Composite

Sunflower Family *(Asteraceae, Compositae)*

SHOWY ASTER

Aster conspicuus Lindl. Flat topped or somewhat rounded clumps of blue composite flowers, each blossom 1 to 1½ inches across, with yellow or brownish discs (centers) The leaves are oval to lance-shaped with sharp tips and shallowly toothed margins.

Leaves in the middle of the stem grow larger than those above and below and they do not have petioles. Blooming occurs from mid to late summer. HABITAT: Forest openings and scattered woodland. RANGE: Wyoming and Idaho, north to the Yukon.

ELK THISTLE

Cirsium foliosum (Hook.) DC. This perennial thistle varies considerably from a low, virtually stemless clump to 3 feet tall. The flowers may be white, red or nearly purple and may occur singly or clustered at the top of the stem. The leaves have spine-tipped teeth on the edges as well as woolly hairs. Leaves usually surround and overtop the flowers. The thick edible stem does not taper appreciably. Flowers appear in early to mid summer. HABITAT: Open foothills to mountain meadows to alpine slopes. RANGE: The Rocky Mountains from Arizona and Colorado to the Yukon.

Sunflower Family *(Asteraceae, Compositae)*

FIVEVEIN or NODDING SUNFLOWER

Helianthella quinquenervis (Hook.) Gray. This showy sunflower has several to many stems, 1½ to 3 feet tall, sprouting from a woody horizontal root. The pale yellow flowers open about 3 to 4 inches wide. Both the leaves and ray petals have five veins or nerves. The leaves display a prominent central vein and two curved lateral veins on each side, while the petals each have five parallel veins. Long petioles support the narrowly elliptical basal leaves, but sharp pointed stem leaves grow sessile and smaller upward. It blooms in the summer. HABITAT: Well drained forest edges, open slopes and meadows in the mountains from medium to high elevation. RANGE: Idaho to South Dakota, south to northern Mexico. COMMENT: One other species, *H. uniflora,* grows on the plains of our region.

Sunflower Family *(Asteraceae, Compositae)*

Sunflower Family *(Asteraceae, Compositae)*

WOOLY SUNFLOWER

Eriophyllum lanatum (Pursh) Forbes. Several to many stems sprout in a tuft from a woody root. Solitary flowers about 1 inch in diameter terminate the stems. The ray florets are often two toned; rich yellow on the ends and orange toward the disc. Dense woolly hairs cover the stems and leaves. Blooms from May to August. HABITAT: Forest openings from dry lowlands to subalpine. RANGE: Utah and Wyoming to British Columbia and the Cascades. COMMENT: Ten varieties cause wide variability in this species.

Sunflower Family *(Asteraceae, Compositae)*

ORANGE HAWKWEED, Devil's Paintbrush

Hieracium aurantiacum L. These unique reddish-orange flowers form tight clusters. Stiff black hairs cover the leaves, buds and stems, which rise 10 to 20 inches tall. Narrow elliptical leaves create a basal rosette. The plants spread extensively from underground roots and may become weedy pests. Blooms in June and July. HABITAT: Roadsides in mountains, fields and open woods, most commonly on disturbed ground. RANGE: A native of Europe and widely scattered across North America.

BLACK EYED SUSAN

Rudbeckia hirta L. These biennial or short lived perennials stand 1 to 3 feet tall, the stems simple or sparingly branched. Solitary blossoms terminate the stems. From eight to twenty yellow or orange ray florets surround a conical or hemispheric disc that is dark purple, brown or black. The narrow lance-shaped leaves rest on long petioles at the base, but are sessile on the stem. Dense hairs cover both stems and leaves. Blooming occurs in summer. HABITAT: Open prairies to scattered forest at moderately high elevations. RANGE: Most of the U.S. and southern Canada. COMMENT: This species has been widely planted in flower gardens and has extended its wild range from eastern and central North America to the Pacific Coast.

Sunflower Family *(Asteraceae, Compositae)*

Sunflower Family *(Asteraceae, Compositae)*

BLACK HEADED (WESTERN) CONEFLOWER

Rudbeckia occidentalis Nutt. A large tubular or cone-shaped head of disc flowers only—ray flowers lacking. These coarse plants, 2 to 6 feet tall, sometimes grow in dense patches. The leaves are large and broad, tapering to sharp points. The flowers appear from June to August. HABITAT: Moist woods, meadows and stream banks to medium elevation in the mountains. RANGE: Montana to Utah and west to the Pacific Coast. COMMENT: This distinctive wildflower should not be mistaken for any other.

33

Sunflower Family *(Asteraceae, Compositae)*　　**Sunflower Family** *(Asteraceae, Compositae)*

CANADA GOLDENROD

Solidago canadensis L. Conical or rounded masses of tiny yellow flowers crowd the top of stems 1 to 4 feet or more. The floral branches may or may not curve and the flowers may all be on one side of the branches. By the time flowers appear in mid to late summer, the lower leaves usually have dropped off. Stem leaves, narrowly lance-shaped, crowd the upper stem. HABITAT: Open woods, roadsides and meadows from low elevation to high in the mountains. RANGE: Canada and Alaska south of the arctic and most of the United States. COMMENT: About a dozen species of goldenrod frequent the Rockies. This one is easily mistaken for Smooth Goldenrod, *S. gigantea.*

WHITE RAYED MULESEARS

Wyethia helianthoides Nutt. These white or creamy flowers, 2^1/$_2$ to 3 inches across, sometimes turn pale yellow in age. They grow in lush low clumps with large elliptic basal leaves to 1 foot long, usually smooth on the edges. Stem leaves are much smaller. The flowers appear in May and June. HABITAT: Moist meadows, woods and stream banks at medium to subalpine elevations. RANGE: E Oregon to S Montana, Wyoming and N Nevada. COMMENT: One may encounter Northern Mulesears, a yellow species, more frequently in the Rockies.

Barberry Family *(Berberidaceae)*

LOW (CREEPING) OREGON GRAPE

Berberis repens Lindl. This low spreading shrub may reproduce by runners or stolons that sprout where they touch the ground. The pinnately compound leaves have five or seven smooth, spine tipped leaflets that resemble holly leaves. Clusters of small bright yellow flowers nestle near the ground from March to June. In the fall Low Oregon Grape produces small, blue edible berries that make a delicately flavored jelly. HABITAT: Deep forest to scattered woods at low to medium elevation. RANGE: Alberta to New Mexico on both sides of the Rockies. COMMENT: A close relative, Tall Oregon Grape, *B. aquifolium,* is the state flower of Oregon. It frequents the valleys and mountains of W Oregon and Washington and is important horticulturally.

Birch Family *(Betulaceae)*

SITKA ALDER, Scrub Alder
Alnus sinuata (Regel) Rydb.
This shrub, 4 to 12 feet high, sometimes makes dense clumps or thickets. Two kinds of flower catkins occur; the male (staminate) flowers, 1 to 2 inches long, hang pendulously, while the shorter female (pistillate) flowers stand upright (see the photograph). The catkins develop as the leaves emerge in the spring on the growth of the current year. The oval leaves, 1½ to 4 inches long, possess fine teeth on the margins and sharp tips. HABITAT: Stream banks and woods to moist, open slopes in the mountains. RANGE: Alaska to Colorado and N California. COMMENT: Alders and birches are closely related and one can easily confuse the two. The fruiting catkins of birches disintegrate when mature, while those of alder remain intact like tiny pine cones.

Borage Family *(Boraginaceae)*

Borage Family *(Boraginaceae)*

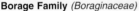

BLUE FORGET-ME-NOT, Jessica's Stickseed

Hackelia micrantha (Eastw.) Gentry. Small round eyes in white or yellow mark the centers of these brilliant blue, open faced flowers, about ¼ inch across. They cluster near the ends of stems and short upper branches. The plant usually produces a clump of stems 1 to 3 feet tall, bearing narrow pointed leaves. Dense hairs cover the stems and leaves. The seeds of *Hackelia* are notoriously prickly, sticking to clothing and animal fur for transportation to new growing sites. Blooms in early to mid summer. HABITAT: Moist meadows and stream banks to scattered timber and open slopes in the mountains. RANGE: Utah and W Wyoming to N California, north to S Alberta and British Columbia. COMMENT: Many Flowered Stickseed closely resembles this one as well as two other species with blue flowers. Four other genera in the borage family are sometimes called forget-me-nots.

BROADLEAVED (TALL) BLUEBELL

Mertensia ciliata (Torr.) G. Don. These lush plants produce numerous stems, 1½ to 3 feet tall or more and clusters of pretty bluebells on the stem ends. The flowers have two sections; the tube and the bell, which are about the same length. The oval- or lance-shaped leaves have fairly long petioles at the base, but grow smaller and sessile upward. Look for these stately plants to bloom from early to mid summer. HABITAT: Moist places from valley bottoms to alpine cirques. RANGE: Colorado to California and north to W Montana. COMMENT: We have ten species of *Mertensia* in the Rockies, three of them tall plants similar to this one.

Honeysuckle Family *(Caprifoliaceae)*

TWINFLOWER

Linnaea borealis L. Slender woody branches lie prostrate, often creating extensive carpets on the mossy forest floor. Short leafy stems stand erect at frequent nodes, topped by pairs of dainty flowers on slender peduncles. The blossoms begin as narrow tubes but flare to five-pointed trumpets. They are white, pink or sometimes rose colored and hairy within. They bloom in the summer. HABITAT: Commonly found in moist, dense forest to scattered woods. RANGE: The northern hemisphere from polar regions south to California, New Mexico and West Virginia. COMMENT: One can easily introduce Twinflower to moist shady gardens. It spreads rapidly providing attractive ground cover. Named for Carl Linnaeus, father of modern botanical taxonomy.

Honeysuckle Family *(Caprifoliaceae)*

ORANGE HONEYSUCKLE

Lonicera ciliosa (Pursh) DC. Bright orange tubular trumpets cluster on the ends of woody climbing vines. The leaves are opposite and broadly oval, except that the pair of leaves just below the flowers are fused at the base and completely encircle the floral stem. Often climbing to heights of 15 to 30 feet, the vines use trees, shrubs and fences for support. Red or orange berries develop in late summer, ordinarily three or four to a cluster. They are seedy, pulpy and edible, but not very tasty. Blooms from May to July. HABITAT: Deep forest to open woods at low to middle elevations in the mountains. RANGE: W Montana to the Pacific Coast.

Honeysuckle Family *(Caprifoliaceae)*   **Honeysuckle Family** *(Caprifoliaceae)*

BLACK TWINBERRY, Bush Honeysuckle

Lonicera involucrata (Rich.) Banks. A pair of fused yellow tubular flowers sit upon two pairs of sticky leafy bracts that turn dark red or purple with age. The elliptical leaves are pointed on the ends and opposite on the stems of this shrub, which grows 3 to 6 feet or more. The fruit consists of pairs of black round berries, joined at the base and still subtended by the colorful bracts. Look for the blooms from April to July. HABITAT: Stream banks to moist woods from the coast to high montane. RANGE: Western North America from S Alaska to Mexico. Occasional in E Canada and northeastern U.S. COMMENT: Black Twinberry fruit is reported to be both edible and poisonous by different authors. The tempting appearance of the berries belies their bitter flavor.

RED TWINBERRY

Lonicera utahensis Wats. A pleasing shrub, 2 to 6 feet tall, with luxuriant oval leaves. The cream or pale yellowish blossoms, sometimes tinged with red, grow in pairs attached at the base. The five petals unite in a tube about $1/2$ inch long and flare prettily at the throat. Bright red watery berries join together in pairs and develop in mid to late summer. HABITAT: Scattered woods to fairly dense forest, usually on well drained soils at medium to subalpine elevations. RANGE: Utah to N California and north into Canada.

Honeysuckle Family *(Caprifoliaceae)*   Honeysuckle Family *(Caprifoliaceae)*

BLACK ELDERBERRY,
Red Berried Elder

Sambucus racemosa L. Conical or round-topped clusters, 3 to 6 inches across, of tiny white flowers embellish a bushy shrub. The stem and twigs are thick but quite brittle and pithy. The pinnately compound leaves consist of five or seven lance-shaped leaflets with sharp indentations or teeth on the margins. The fruit develop into a rounded mass of dark red to black edible, but seedy berries. Flowers bloom from May to July. HABITAT: Moist woods and forest openings in the mountains. RANGE: Hemispheric, south in the mountains to New Mexico, Arizona and California. COMMENT: Blue Elderberry bears flowers and fruit in flat-topped clusters. Home winemakers prize the berries.

MOUNTAIN SNOWBERRY

Symphoricarpos oreophilus Gray. Clusters of white waxy berries dot the upper stems of branching shrubs 2 to 4 feet high in late summer and most of the winter. Birds and rodents feed on the berries reluctantly. The small smooth leaves, opposite on the stems, vary from narrow to oval in outline. The white or pinkish flowers, about $1/3$ inch long, are narrowly tubular or bell-shaped. They bloom from early to mid summer. HABITAT: Well drained soils in the mountains. RANGE: Southwestern Canada to Montana and northern Mexico east of the Cascade crest. COMMENT: Three other species of snowberry in the Rockies display smaller, shorter flowers.

Pink Family *(Caryophyllaceae)*

Stafftree Family *(Celastraceae)*

PARRY'S CATCHFLY

Silene parryi (Wats.) Hitchc. & Mag. These rather captivating wildflowers have large cupped or somewhat inflated calyces (united sepals) decorated with prominent purple stripes. Each white petal protrudes from the calyx with four rounded lobes on the end. Look for these blooms in mid summer. HABITAT: In the mountains from moderate to subalpine elevation. RANGE: British Columbia, south to W Wyoming and W Washington. COMMENT: We have a dozen or so species of catchfly in the Rockies, several introduced and weedy.

MOUNTAIN LOVER, Mountain Box

Pachistima myrsinites (Pursh) Raf. These dense low shrubs bear lustrous evergreen leaves about 1 inch long, sharply toothed on the margins. Tiny maroon, 4-petaled flowers grow one or more in the axils of the sessile leaves. Look for these little jewels from May into June. HABITAT: Common at medium to lower levels in the mountains and woodlands, preferring open to moderately dense forest. RANGE: Southern British Columbia and Alberta south to California and New Mexico. COMMENT: Mountain Lover makes excellent low shrubbery plantings and Christmas greenery. It provides important winter forage for game animals.

Dogwood Family *(Cornaceae)*

Dogwood Family *(Cornaceae)*

BUNCHBERRY, Dwarf Cornel

Cornus canadensis L. Low spreading plants make excellent ground cover. They display four stylish white bracts, about 1 inch long, oval in outline and pointed on the ends. These bracts are really specialized leafy scales. The minute flowers, arranged in a tight cluster above the base of the bracts, possess pretty purple centers. Larger than the bracts, bright green and the same general shape, the leaves form a whorl, four to six in number, below the bracts. The fruit emerge in late summer as a bunch of small red drupes that look like berries, edible but rather tasteless. Blooming occurs in June and July. HABITAT: Common in moist woods from low to mid elevations. RANGE: Asia and arctic America, south through the Rockies.

REDOSIER DOGWOOD

Cornus stolonifera Michx. These spreading shrubs often form thickets, 3 to 6 feet high, with bright red bark on stems and twigs that one notices especially in winter. The small flowers appear in a tight, flat topped white cluster. The fruit develop into a bunch of bluish white waxy drupes with single stones. It blooms principally in June. HABITAT: Stream banks and other wet places. RANGE: Most of North America. COMMENT: Early pioneers used the inner bark as a substitute for tobacco.

Oleaster Family *(Eleagnaceae)*

CANADA BUFFALO BERRY, Soapberry

Shepherdia canadensis (L.) Nutt. This pleasingly bushy shrub grows 3 to 12 feet tall. The simple, opposite leaves are bright green above with noticeable veins but covered with grey or brownish scales on the under side. One can easily overlook the tiny brownish unisexual flowers in the leaf axils, but the fruit are quite attractive, becoming yellow or red oval berries. They have a bitter taste but can be used in making jelly. Blooms before or as the leaves expand. HABITAT: Deep woods to open areas or forest fringes. RANGE: Transcontinental; Oregon northward and eastward. Common in the Rockies. COMMENT: *S. argentaea,* another species in the Rocky Mountains bears thorns and narrower leaves.

FOOL'S HUCKLEBERRY

Menziesia ferruginea Smith. Yellowish pink, urn-shaped flowers, about ¼ inch long, they grow in clusters of three or four at the ends of the previous years' growth. These shrubs stand 4 to 6 feet high and often make dense understories in coniferous woods. The leaves are oval in outline, short petioled and about 1½ to 2 inches long, turning red or yellow in the autumn. They bloom from May to August. HABITAT: Moist woods from medium to subalpine reaches. RANGE: The Rocky Mountains from Canada to Wyoming and the Columbia River gorge. COMMENT: Another variety grows commonly along the Pacific Coast from Alaska to N California.

Heath Family *(Ericaceae)*

44

Heath Family *(Ericaceae)*

CANDY STICK

Allotropa virgata T. & G. Exquisite spikes, 4 to 16 inches tall, decorated with stark white and bright pink or red longitudinal stripes. The small maroon flowers lack petals and nestle in the axils of white leaf-like scales. This plant is a saprophyte and blooms in summer, commonly following a soaking rain.

HABITAT: Low to high montane forests. RANGE: Cascade-Sierra and Coast Ranges from British Columbia to California. In the Rockies, a limited area centered on the Bitterroot Mountains of west-central Montana and adjacent Idaho in lodgepole pine forests. COMMENT: *Allotropa* has just one species.

45

KINNIKINNIK, Bearberry

Arctostaphylos uva-ursi (L.) Spreng.
Small urn-shaped flowers, white to
pink, bunch on the ends of branches.
This prostrate shrub often forms
extensive carpets on the forest floor.
The leaves are evergreen, waxy
smooth, oval and about 1 inch long.
Edible red berries replace the flowers in
mid to late summer, but they are hard,
pulpy and seedy. The flowers open in
late spring. HABITAT: Dense to open
woods and forest edges. RANGE:
Circumpolar in the northern
hemisphere. COMMENT: Kinnikinnik is
very common in the forests of the
Rockies. We have three species and
they all make excellent ground cover in
shady places.

Heath Family *(Ericaceae)*

Heath Family *(Ericaceae)*

PIPSISSEWA, Prince's Pine

Chimaphila umbellata (L.) Bart.
Five pink to rose petals open widely
surrounding a prominent green ovary.
Several of these charming, nodding
flowers decorate stem ends. The plant
is a low spreading evergreen semi-
shrub. Leathery leaves, arranged in
one or two whorls below the flowers,
display small sharp teeth on the
margins. It blooms early in the summer.
HABITAT: Coniferous woods where
moist in the spring. RANGE: Temperate
forests of the northern hemisphere,
south to Colorado.

46

Heath Family *(Ericaceae)*

AMERICAN PINESAP
Hypopitys monotropa Crantz.
This saprophyte lacks green leaves and consequently lives on decayed organic material in the soil. Unbranched stems, red to yellowish tinged, stand 10 inches high or less. The flowers nod and emerge from the axils of leaf-like scales, creating spiky racemes. They bloom from June to August.

HABITAT: Forest duff from low elevation to subalpine heights. RANGE: Across North America and in Europe. COMMENT: Just one species occurs in our region, but several others are recognized in eastern United States and in Europe. Pinesap, though wide ranging, is not common and appears endangered in Colorado.

Heath Family *(Ericaceae)*

Heath Family *(Ericaceae)*

INDIAN PIPE

Monotropa uniflora L. Waxy white stems sprout in clumps, grow to 10 inches high and bear a single pendent flower atop each stem. This saprophyte lacks green leaves and turns black and upright with age. The flowers appear in mid to late summer, usually following a soaking rain. HABITAT: Dense moist woods. RANGE: Temperate North America. COMMENT: In years of plentiful summer rain, Indian Pipe may be locally abundant.

PINEDROPS

Pterospora andromedea Nutt. This reddish or yellowish brown saprophyte, lacking green leaves, lifts unbranched stems 1 to 3 feet high. It lives on decayed organic matter in the forest floor. The flowers are about $1/2$ inch long, urn-shaped or bell-shaped and numerous. They droop from slender pedicels in the axils of scaly bracts. Look for these unusual plants in the summer. HABITAT: Deep woods to open forests at low to moderate elevations. RANGE: Mountainous North America. COMMENT: Although Pinedrops range widely, they seldom occur very abundantly.

Buttercup Family *(Ranunculaceae)*   **Buttercup Family** *(Ranunculaceae)*

MONKSHOOD

Aconitum columbianum Nutt. This
conspicuously distinctive flower, about
1½ inches from top to bottom, has five
showy sepals. The upper one forms a
hood or helmet with a pointed beak.
Two other fan-shaped sepals spread
wide on the sides and the lower two
are narrow and less showy. Two or
sometimes five small petals blend with
the sepals and tend to disappear.
Bright blue or purple flowers
predominate, but one may find a cream
colored variety in E Oregon and
Washington. These tall plants, 3 to 7
feet, have broad, palmately divided and
toothed leaves. Blooms appear in early
summer. HABITAT: Moist woods or
forest fringes from low to subalpine
elevations. RANGE: Forested areas of
western U.S. and Canada. COMMENT:
Aconitin, a chemical especially
prevalent in the seeds and roots,
makes monkshood very poisonous.

PURPLE VIRGIN'S BOWER,
Rock Clematis

Clematis columbiana (Nutt.) T. & G.
These solitary, pale blue or purple
flowers possess four or sometimes five
lance-shaped sepals (no petals), 1½ to
2½ inches long, that droop stylishly.
Many white or yellow stamens crowd
the center of the blossoms. The leaves
have three well spaced leaflets, lance-
shaped and indented on the margins
but not lobed. The tiny seeds have long
feathery plumes that drift on the wind.
These woody vines creep along the
ground in forests or on steep rocky
slopes with scant cover. They bloom in
May and June. HABITAT: Valleys and
mid elevation woods to near alpine.
RANGE: British Columbia and Alberta
to Colorado.

Flower, Buttercup Family *(Ranunculaceae)*

Fruit, Buttercup Family *(Ranunculaceae)*

BANEBERRY

Actaea rubra (Ait.) Willd. A tight, nearly spherical raceme of small white flowers with many bristling stamens to catch the eye. This perennial herb usually branches and bears only a few very large leaves. The basal leaves clasp the stem and may branch three times pinnately Leaflets in threes have irregularly toothed margins. Round berries, either bright waxy red or white and reportedly poisonous, develop in mid to late summer. Blooms mostly in May and June. HABITAT: Moist woods, fairly open to quite dense. RANGE: Most of temperate North America. COMMENT: Might be confused with False Bugbane, p. 69.

Buttercup Family (*Ranunculaceae*)

WINDFLOWER

Anemone piperi Britt. Lovely white or delicate pink anemones provide a tonic for the spirits soon after spring arrives. Windflower normally has five showy sepals, but sometimes one finds a "double" with ten sepals. A mound of greenish white stamens decorates the center of the blossom. Three leaves in a whorl, each with three toothed leaflets, circle the stem just below the flower. Look for these gay jewels from April to June. HABITAT: Wooded canyon bottoms and damp forests. RANGE: E Oregon and Washington to W Montana.

WESTERN MEADOWRUE

Thalictrum occidentale Gray. This species has male (staminate) flowers and female (pistillate) flowers on separate plants. One more easily notices the staminate flowers, which consist of masses of pendulous yellow stamens, about ⅛ inch long, hanging on slender, brownish purple filaments as shown in the photo. Small papery sepals (no petals) make tiny umbrellas above the flowers. The pistillate flowers are inconspicuous, green or purplish burr-like heads of naked ovaries (upper left in the photo). Large leaves clasp the stem at the base and divide or branch two to four times. Shiny leaflets, about 1 inch across, are rounded and normally three lobed. The lobes in turn have rounded scallops. Blooms May to July. HABITAT: Woods and meadows. RANGE: Colorado and Utah to Canada and the Cascades. COMMENT: We have six species of meadowrue in the Rockies.

Buttercup Family (*Ranunculaceae*)

Buttercup Family *(Ranunculaceae)*

GOLDEN COLUMBINE

Aquilegia flavescens Wats. A striking columbine in red and yellow. Five petals, attached near their middles, have rounded lobes below and become long, curling tubes or spurs above. The petals alternate with five similarly colored sepals. A multitude of stamens protrude from the floral center. The leaves, mostly basal, divide twice into threes, the leaflets rounded and lobed. Blooms late spring and early summer. HABITAT: Open woods or fringes, commonly to subalpine. RANGE: Utah and W Colorado to southern British Columbia and Alberta. COMMENT: Columbine comes from the Italian word "colombo," meaning dove. Note the family of doves in the flower. The red tinted specimen shown here is unusual, because most plants of this species bear all yellow flowers. Red Columbine, *A. formosa,* typically presents this combination of colors in our area, but the incurling spurs (instead of straight ones) identify this species.

Buttercup Family *(Ranunculaceae)*

Buckthorn Family *(Rhamnaceae)*

FALSE BUGBANE

Trautvetteria caroliniensis (Walt.) Vail. Flat-topped masses of showy, greenish white flowers perch on top of stems 1½ to 3 feet tall. Each blossom has four or more small linear sepals and numerous stamens about ¼ inch long. The attractive leaves are palmately lobed, like maple leaves, 4 to 10 inches broad and toothed on the margins. They sprout mostly from the base of the plant. Blooms appear from May to July. HABITAT: Damp ground in the woods. RANGE: British Columbia south to New Mexico and California, central and eastern U.S. and Japan. COMMENT: Widely scattered and not very common in the Rockies. See Baneberry, p. 66.

BUCKBRUSH, Redstem Ceanothus

Ceanothus sanguineus Pursh. Dense clusters of tiny white flowers bloom on the ends of short side branches of the previous years' growth. These shrubs grow 3 to 10 feet, the bark a pretty dark red to brownish purple. Alternate leaves are 1 to 3 inches long, broadly oval with fine teeth on the margins. The flowers bloom from May to July. HABITAT: Open to dense forest or clearings in the woods. RANGE: Montana, west to the coast, British Columbia to California. COMMENT: Another species, *Ceanothus velutinus,* grows low to the ground, bears evergreen leaves and ranges from Colorado and California north into Canada. Big game animals browse heavily on both species, especially in winter.

Rose Family *(Rosaceae)*

Rose Family *(Rosaceae)*

SERVICEBERRY, Shadbush

Amelanchier alnifolia Nutt. These cheerful white flowers have five narrow petals, $1/2$ to $3/4$ inch long, and ten to twenty stamens growing in a few-flowered raceme on branch ends. The plant is a shrub. The oval leaves, 1 to 2 inches long, vary from smooth on the edges to finely toothed. The fruit consist of edible but rather mealy berries, which Indians used extensively in the early days for making pemmican. They bloom from April to June or July. HABITAT: Open to fairly dense woods. RANGE: Western mountains north of Mexico. COMMENT: Utah serviceberry, a smaller shrub, commonly is present on the plains and prairies.

CLIFF ROSE, Quinine Bush

Cowania mexicana. Glorious flowering shrubs, 4 to 12 feet tall, may be gnarled and stunted in exposed places but robust and luxuriant on more protected sites. The pale yellow petals and bright yellow stamens, similar to apple blossoms, cover branch ends and give off a lovely fragrance. Several tiny three- to seven-lobed, evergreen leaves sprout from short spurs along the limbs. The fruit are small hard seeds with silky tails. Blooms persist from May to August. HABITAT: Dry scrub or brush zone to lower montane forest. RANGE: Utah and W Colorado, south in the mountains.

Rose Family *(Rosaceae)*

BIRCHLEAF MOUNTAIN MAHOGANY
Cercocarpus montanus Raf. Shrubs or small trees, heavily branched with many short stubby side branches, sometimes form rather extensive forests. The leaves are evergreen for two or three years and oval with conspicuous veins. One to three sessile flowers emerge from the leaf axils arising on short spurs. The petals roll backward, forming shallow cups about ¼ inch across. The small hard seed has a plumy tail. Blooms in spring. HABITAT: Dry rocky hillsides or in scattered timber. RANGE: Wyoming to Mexico and west to the coast.

Rose Family *(Rosaceae)*

BLACK HAWTHORN,
River Hawthorn, Thornapple
Crataegus douglasii Lindl., *Crataegus rivularis* (Nutt.) Sarg. A large spreading shrub or small tree, armed with stout thorns about an inch long. The flowers usually have five white rounded petals and ten to twenty stamens. The flowers create showy clusters on branch ends and in leaf axils. Small dry seedy apples or haws develop in the fall. Birds and small animals feed on them in the winter. The flowers appear in May and June. HABITAT: Stream banks and open woods with deep soil. RANGE: S Alaska to Alberta and Colorado, Utah and California.

DUSKY HORKELIA

Horkelia fusca Lindl. Five wide spreading petals are narrow at the base and idented at the tips, white to pink with red lines. These pleasing flowers crowd the top of several unbranched stems, 6 to 20 inches tall. Five reddish sepals, copiously hairy, clothe the unopened buds. Leaves to 8 inches long are pinnately compound, the leaflets divided and lobed irregularly with three to eleven pointed or slightly rounded segments. Look for them from June to August. HABITAT: Grassy meadows and scattered timber in the mountains. RANGE: Wyoming, Idaho and Nevada, west to the Cascades and Sierras. COMMENT: Seventeen species of *Horkelia* can be found in California, but only this one beautifies the Rockies.

Rose Family *(Rosaceae)*

Rose Family *(Rosaceae)*

WILD STRAWBERRY

Fragaria virginiana Duchesne. Low perennial herbs, 3 or 4 inches high, they commonly spread by long slender runners or stolons that usually have a red tinge. The white flowers grow in clusters of two or more on slender peduncles 2 to 6 inches long. Blooms occur from May to mid summer. Small, sweet juicy strawberries develop by mid to late summer. HABITAT: Open grassy meadows to moderately dense woods from low to medium elevation. RANGE: Transcontinental. Common in eastern U.S. and south to Colorado. COMMENT: Two species of wild strawberry inhabit the Rocky Mountains.

NINEBARK

Physocarpus malvaceus (Greene) Kuntze. This decorative shrub grows 2 to 6 feet tall, sometimes making dense thickets. The outer bark on older stems shreds and strips off easily. The flowers form charming spherical clusters of white petals, accented by brownish yellow centers and protruding stamens. The leaves are palmately lobed, generally three times or more, and toothed on the edges. Blooming takes place in early summer. HABITAT: Open coniferous forests, preferring fairly steep slopes. RANGE: Southern British Columbia and Alberta to Utah and Wyoming.

Rose Family *(Rosaceae)*

Rose Family *(Rosaceae)*

OCEAN SPRAY, Mountain Spray

Holodiscus discolor (Pursh) Maxim. These shrubs, 2 to 10 feet tall, produce glorious pyramidal sprays of tiny white flowers. Many stems curve gracefully outward on large plants under the weight of masses of bloom. Numerous shallow scallops grace the margins of the oval or triangular leaves. Blooms in midsummer. HABITAT: Well drained or rocky soil in the mountains. RANGE: Montana to British Columbia and California. COMMENT: From Idaho southward one finds a smaller species, *H. dumosus.*

73

MARSH CINQUEFOIL,
Purple Cinquefoil

Potentilla palustris (L.) Scop. A low prostrate creeper with red or purplish stems up to 3 feet long that root by layering at frequent nodes. Clasping the stem with long petioles, the pinnate leaves have five or seven sharply toothed leaflets, 1 to 2 inches long. The open faced flowers display five petals and five sepals, all sharp pointed and ordinarily about the same length, but the dark red to purple petals are usually broader than the sepals. It blooms the first half of summer. HABITAT: Wet meadows, marshes and lake or stream banks from low to high elevations. RANGE: Boreal forests across North America and south in the Rockies to Wyoming.

Rose Family *(Rosaceae)*

Rose Family *(Rosaceae)*

STICKY CINQUEFOIL

Potentilla glandulosa Lindl. The flowers of this attractive species vary from bright lemon yellow to cream, attributable to five varieties. Furthermore, a similar species, *P. arguta*, closely resembles this pale variety. "Cinquefoil" means five leaves or petals. The leaves have five to nine pinnate leaflets, sharply toothed. Sticky glandular hairs cover the stems and leaves. Blooms from May to early July. HABITAT: Rocky places in the mountains and prairies. RANGE: Arizona to Baja and north into Canada.

74

Rose Family *(Rosaceae)*

WILD PLUM

Prunus americana Marsh. These shrubs or small trees sometimes create dense thickets. The blossoms cluster near branch ends below terminal leaves. Stubby side branches often have narrow tips, and become quite thorny. The leaves are elliptical, 2 to 4 inches long, sharp pointed and toothed on the margins. Small orange to purple plums with flattened pits develop in mid to late summer. They bloom in the spring. HABITAT: Wooded stream banks and open forests with deep soil. RANGE: Montana to Utah and Arizona and east across the continent. COMMENT: The flowers could be mistaken for two species of wild cherry.

PRICKLY ROSE

Rosa acicularis Lindl. Many sharp straight prickles of varying length cover the stems of this beautiful wild rose, the floral emblem of Alberta. The elegant pink blossoms, about 2 inches broad, occur singly on new growth of the current year. The plants stand 1 to 5 feet tall and bear pinnately compound leaves with five or seven elliptical leaflets sharply toothed on the margins. Fine sticky hairs often line the sides of the teeth. Blooms in late spring and early summer. HABITAT: Woods and forest fringes. RANGE: Circumpolar, south in the mountains to New Mexico. COMMENT: Rose hips, though mealy and seedy, are rich in vitamins and make a potable wine. Many birds and animals feed on them in winter.

Rose Family *(Rosaceae)*

Rose Family *(Rosaceae)*

WOOD'S ROSE, Wild Rose

Rosa woodsii Lindl. Wood's Rose generally has fewer thorns than Prickly Rose, commonly only two at the base of each leaf. They may or may not curve and some usually have thick bases. In most other respects the two species appear very similar. Blooms from May to July. HABITAT: One variety, *woodsii,* inhabits the Great Plains, while var. *ultramontana* prefers moist woods and stream banks in the mountains. RANGE: Northcentral Canada to S California, east to Missouri and Wisconsin.

BOULDER RASPBERRY

Rubus deliciosus James. Spectacular flowers, 2 to 3 inches in diameter, with five nearly translucent white petals. Many yellowish brown stamens crowd the center. This shrub sends up several stems to 5 feet tall, the bark of the new growth is quite reddish. The leaves are round to oval, about 2 inches long, prominently veined, with irregular lobes and many sharp teeth on the margins. Fruit is a small raspberry and decidedly not delicious. Look for it to bloom in May. HABITAT: Open forests in the foothills and mesas. RANGE: Limited to Wyoming and Colorado. COMMENT: The largest raspberry blossoms and a good horticultural prospect. A similar species with slightly smaller flowers, *R. neomexicana,* occurs farther south.

Rose Family *(Rosaceae)*

Rose Family *(Rosaceae)*

THIMBLEBERRY

Rubus parviflorus Nutt. These common shrubs grow in patches, spreading from underground roots. The stems usually rise 2 to 4 feet and do not branch below the crown. The inflorescence does branch ordinarily with three or four blossoms or a few more. Broad, palmately lobed leaves dwarf the white or occasionally pink flowers. The raspberries have a mealy, insipid taste. They bloom from May to July. HABITAT: Low to high in the mountains in scattered to dense forest. RANGE: Alaska to Mexico and east to the Great Lakes.

STEEPLEBUSH

Spiraea douglasii Hook. This stunning shrub branches often, stands 2 to 6 feet tall and presents shiny oval leaves. Masses of tiny pink to bright rose flowers compose the elongated, pyramidal inflorescense. Look for this beauty in the summer. HABITAT: It flourishes on stream banks and other wet or boggy sites from the coast to subalpine. RANGE: Idaho and peripheral areas of adjacent states, north to Alaska.

Rose Family *(Rosaceae)*

Rose Family *(Rosaceae)*

BIRCHLEAF SPIRAEA

Spiraea betulifolia Pall. Low shrubs, 10 to 20 inches tall, they spread widely from strong underground roots. A dense flat-topped cluster of tiny white to pale pink flowers, that appear fuzzy from many protruding stamens, top the unbranched stems. The oval, alternate leaves, 1 to 2 inches long and toothed on the ends, resemble the leaves of birch trees. The blooms open in early to mid summer. HABITAT: Scattered to dense forest from low to subalpine. RANGE: Western Canada to Oregon and Wyoming and in Asia.

Rose Family *(Rosaceae)*

Madder Family *(Rubiaceae)*

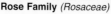

CASCADE MOUNTAIN ASH (berries)

Sorbus scopulina Greene. This aesthetic shrub likes steep mountainsides, where it often forms dense patches. Winter snows commonly bend the stems downhill near the base. A multitude of small white flowers create dense, flat topped clusters to 6 inches broad on branch ends. The leaves have 9 to 13 pinnate leaflets, pointed on the end and sharply toothed. Blooms in early summer. HABITAT: Woods and cutover land in the mountains. RANGE: Alaska to New Mexico and N California. COMMENT: Sitka Mountain Ash, *S. sitchensis,* has rounded leaflets and ranges south to Oregon and Montana. Birds, especially waxwings, and animals dine on the orange berries in winter.

FRAGRANT BEDSTRAW

Galium boreale L. Masses of tiny white flowers grace this perennial, 10 to 30 inches high. It grows in clumps, spreading from underground roots. Five or six narrow pointed leaves make a whorl at each lower stem node, while the upper nodes usually have just two opposite leaves. Look for bedstraw to bloom from June to August. HABITAT: Moist woods and clearings. RANGE: Circumboreal (the northern hemisphere), extending south to Florida and Mexico. COMMENT: We have eight species in the Rockies, all quite similar in appearance.

Saxifrage Family *(Saxifragaceae)*

Saxifrage Family *(Saxifragaceae)*

ROUNDLEAF ALUMROOT
Heuchera cylindrica Dougl. Cup-shaped
flowers ¼ to ⅓ inch long crowd the end
of slender, naked stems 6 to 36 inches
tall. Short peduncles, that may branch
close to the stem, support the flowers.
Five cream or greenish, overlapping
sepals compose the floral cups. Petals
may be lacking, but if present, they
hide within the cups. The leaves, all
basal, are generally round in outline
and scalloped with shallow lobes. It
blooms from mid spring to mid summer.
HABITAT: Gravelly or rocky soil, rock
slides or rock crevices. RANGE:
Southern British Columbia and Alberta
south to Wyoming and NE California.
COMMENT: A half dozen species of
Heuchera inhabit our region.

BREWER'S MITREWORT,
Bishop's Cap
Mitella breweri Gray. Five rounded
sepals, barely visible, support a little,
round, yellowish green saucer about ⅛
inch across. The five ornamental petals
divide pinnately into five to nine
threadlike lobes, which make the
flowers look like snow flakes. Rising
from spreading rhizomes, the naked,
unbranched stems stand 6 to 12 inches
high. Many irregular teeth or shallow
lobes mark the margins of the roundly
heart-shaped or kidney-shaped basal
leaves. Blooms from May to August,
depending on elevation. HABITAT:
Moist, often mossy places in the woods
from low elevation to subalpine heights.
RANGE: W Montana, N Idaho and S
Alberta, west to the coast, British
Columbia to California.

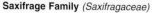

Saxifrage Family *(Saxifragaceae)*

Saxifrage Family *(Saxifragaceae)*

SIDE FLOWERED MITREWORT, Sleighbells

Mitella stauropetala Piper. These fascinating little flowers all grow on one side of unbranching, leafless stems. The sepals are usually white but occasionally purplish, about ⅛ inch long, and sharply rolled backward forming tiny shallow cups. The petals, also about ⅛ inch, spread widely into cross-shaped, linear lobes, imparting a lacy appearance to the blossoms. The leaves grow in a basal rosette on long hairy petioles, the blades broadly heart-shaped. This delicate plant blooms from mid to late spring. HABITAT: Moist woods in canyon bottoms to near subalpine. RANGE: E Washington to W Montana and south to Utah and Colorado. COMMENT: Six species of *Mitella* occur in the Rockies, all characterized by lacy, lobed petals.

FOAMFLOWER, False Mitrewort

Tiarella trifoliata var. *unifoliata* (Hook.) Kurtz. An open inflorescence of tiny nodding flowers decorate slender branching stems. The calyx and white petals create a shallow, star-shaped cup filled with ten prominently protruding, more or less pendulous stamens. Maple-like leaves, about 4 inches broad, grow on long petioles from the base of the plant and on short petioles on the flowering stems. Look for these captivating little charmers in early to mid summer. HABITAT: Dense forest at medium elevations. RANGE: Montana to California and north to Alaska. COMMENT: Trefoil Foamflower has three-lobed compound leaves, but otherwise appears much the same.

Figwort Family *(Scrophulariaceae)*   **Figwort Family** *(Scrophulariaceae)*

SCARLET PAINTBRUSH

Castilleja miniata Dougl. This is perhaps the most common and widespread Indian paintbrush in our woods and mountains. The resplendent red to crimson, or very occasionally yellow, bracts of the inflorescence catch one's attention immediately. The leaves and bracts are mostly linear or narrowly lance-shaped, but occasional specimens have narrow lateral lobes. One or a few stems rise 10 to 30 inches from a woody root crown. Blooms appear from late spring into summer. HABITAT: Woods and forest openings to mid elevation in the mountains. RANGE: Mountainous regions of western North America, north of Mexico. COMMENT: Like most Indian paintbrushes, this one tends to hybridize and positive species identification can prove difficult.

SULPHUR PAINTBRUSH

Castilleja sulphurea Rydb. A choice yellow or greenish Indian paintbrush that grows in a tuft of numerous stems, 6 to 18 inches high. The leaves and bracts are usually simple and narrow, but at times, one will find upper leaves and bracts with two or four linear, lateral lobes. For the most part the flowers hide behind the bracts and bloom through the summer. HABITAT: Open forest or meadows from the valleys to subalpine. RANGE: Southern Alberta and the Black Hills of South Dakota through the Rockies to New Mexico. COMMENT: This species could easily be mistaken for Slender Indian Paintbrush, shown in Vol. I, *Prairie Wildflowers.*

Figwort Family *(Scrophulariaceae)*

YELLOW MONKEYFLOWER,
Spotted Monkeyflower
Mimulus guttatus DC. A brilliant yellow tube, ½ to 1½ inches long, the flaring lower lip constricts the throat and displays several reddish spots. Highly variable in growth habit, from 3 to 30 inches long and upright or reclining.

The luxuriant leaves are lance- or heart-shaped and sharply indented. Blooms from spring through summer. HABITAT: Moist soil and stream banks. RANGE: Western North America and introduced into many other parts of the world. COMMENT: One could easily mistake this for eight other species.

GRAY'S LOUSEWORT, Indian Warrior
Pedicularis grayi Nels. This stately lousewort stands 2 to 4 feet tall in a clump of elegant fern-like leaves to 1 foot long. The flower is nearly 1½ inches long, pale yellow and delicately decorated with red or purple stripes. An upper petal extends outward and down at the tip in a narrow pointed beak. It nearly touches the broad three lobed lower lip. The flowers erupt from the axils of leaflike bracts, creating an elongated, spiky raceme. Blooms occur in summer. HABITAT: Grassy meadows and open woods from montane to subalpine. RANGE: Utah and Wyoming and south in the mountains.

Figwort Family *(Scrophulariaceae)*

Figwort Family *(Scrophulariaceae)*　　　**Figwort Family** *(Scrophulariaceae)*

**SCORCHED PENSTEMON,
Yellow Beardtongue**

Penstemon confertus Dougl. A tuft of stems 8 to 20 inches tall originates on a perennial root crown. Two or more dense whorl-like clusters of white, cream or yellow flowers form the inflorescence. The blossoms are tubular, ½ inch long or less, flaring to two lips. The lower lip tends to hang downward. Purple stamens afford spots of color in the floral throats. Lance-shaped leaves make a basal rosette and the sessile stem leaves are in opposite pairs. Blooms in late spring to mid summer. HABITAT: Moist, open montane woods or meadows. RANGE: Wyoming to Alberta and west to the Cascades. COMMENT: This one can easily be mistaken for Hot Rock Penstemon, *P. deustus.*

**SHRUBBY PENSTEMON,
Lowbush Penstemon**

Penstemon fruticosus (Pursh) Greene. This gorgeous wildflower has several large blue to purple blossoms, 1 to 1½ inches long, in a raceme that tends to grow on one side of the stem. White hairs impart a light fuzzy texture to the lower lip, which protrudes farther than the upper lip. The plant is a low shrub that may or may not spread and form ground covering mats. Oval or linear, sharply indented or smooth margined, the leaves vary according to the variety. Blossoms emerge from May to August depending on elevation. HABITAT: Rocky or gravelly slopes in the mountains. RANGE: Wyoming to Oregon and north into Canada. COMMENT: Approximately 60 species of *Penstemon* are found in the Rockies.

84

Figgwort Family *(Scrophulariaceae)*

**SMALL FLOWERED PENSTEMON,
Clustered Penstemon**

Penstemon procerus Dougl. Several stems grow in a tuft and one or more dense clusters of small, dark blue or sometimes cream colored flowers terminate the stems. The clusters appear as whorls, but actually grow on short penduncles, originating in leaf axils. Several pairs of opposite leaves, bright green, entire and sessile decorate the stems. Some larger, lance-shaped leaves on petioles may garnish the base of the plant. Look for these engaging beauties in early summer. HABITAT: Well drained slopes and meadows in the mountains. RANGE: Colorado and California to northern Canada and Alaska. COMMENT: Rydberg's Penstemon closely resembles this one.

Figgwort Family *(Scrophulariaceae)*

MOUNTAIN KITTENTAIL

Synthyris missurica (Raf.) Pennell. A dense raceme of brilliant, sky-blue flowers terminate a succulent stem 4 to 20 inches tall. Each bell shaped blossom has four petals, about ¼ inch long, two protruding stamens and one pistil. The leaves are glossy green, roundly heart shaped and deeply scalloped on the edges. Look for this one early, April to June. HABITAT: Moist canyon bottoms and hillsides from low to mid elevations. RANGE: W Montana, Idaho and Washington to California. COMMENT: This species has potential as a valuable perennial for shady gardens. We have 4 species of *Synthyris* in the Rocky Mountains.

Violet Family *(Violaceae)*

EARLY BLUE VIOLET

Viola adunca Sm. These lovely blue violets commonly grow in low clumps, the flower stems branching from a central stem that may be very short and indistinct. Showy white beards and dark purple guide lines usually mark the lower three petals. The lower petal projects backward into a short curved spur. The leaves, mostly basal, are heart shaped. A spring to mid summer bloomer. HABITAT: Moist woods and meadows. RANGE: Most of North America.

Violet Family *(Violaceae)*

CANADA VIOLET
Viola canadensis L. These merry little violets grow from upper leaf axils and display five white or pinkish petals. Pretty purple stripes called guide lines mark the three lower petals and small yellow hairy beards decorate the base of the two lateral petals. Two upper petals usually have purple tinges on the back. Long petioles, to 1 foot, support broadly heart-shaped basal leaves. This native perennial blooms from late spring to mid summer. HABITAT: Damp woods from low to medium elevations. RANGE: Alaska across Canada, most of the East Coast and south through the Rockies to New Mexico and Arizona.

Selected references

1. Booth, W.E. and J.C. Wright. *Flora of Montana, Part II.* Montana State Univ. Bozeman. 1959.

2. Clark, Lewis J. *Wild Flowers of the Pacific Northwest.* Gray's. Sidney. B.C. 1976.

3. Craighead, John J., F.C. Craighead and R.J. Davis. *A Field Guide to Rocky Mountain Wildflowers.* Houghton Mifflin. Cambridge. 1963.

4. Dorn, Robert D. *Vascular Plants of Montana.* Mountain West. Cheyenne. 1984.

5. Harrington. H.D. *Edible Native Plants of the Rocky Mountains.* Univ. of New Mexico. Albuquerque. 1976.

6. Hitchcock. C. Leo, A. Cronquist, M. Ownbey and J.W. Thompson, eds. *Vascular Plants of the Pacific Northwest,* in 5 Vols. Univ. of Wash. Seattle. 1955 to 1969.

7. Hitchcock. C. Leo and A. Cronquist. *Flora of the Pacific Northwest.* Univ. of Wash. Seattle. 1973.

8. Larrison, Earl J., G.W. Patrick. W.H. Baker and J.A. Yaich. *Washington Wildflowers.* Seattle Audubon Soc. 1974.

9. Lesica, P. *Checklist of the Vascular Plants of Glacier National Park.* Montana Acad. of Sci. 1985.

10. Lesica, P. *et al. Vascular Plants of Limited Distribution in Montana.* Montana Acad. of Sci. 1984.

11. Lyons. C.P. *Trees Shrubs and Flowers to Know in Washington.* Evergreen. Vancouver. 1956.

12. McDougall. W.B. and H.A. Baggley. *The Plants of Yellowstone National Park.* Wheelwright. 1956.

13. Moss. E.H. *Flora of Alberta.* Univ. of Toronto. 1959.

14. Nelson. Burrell E. *Vascular Plants of the Medicine Bow Range.* Jelm Mtn. Press. Laramie. 1984.

15. Nelson. Ruth A. *Handbook of Rocky Mountain Plants.* D.S. King. Tucson. 1969.

16. Niehaus, T.F. and C.L. Ripper. *A Field Guide to Pacific States Wildflowers.* Houghton Mifflin. Boston. 1976.

17. Orr, R.T. and M.C. Orr. *Wildflowers of Western America.* Galahad. N.Y. 1981.

18. Shaw. R.J. and D. On. *Plants of Waterton-Glacier National Parks.* Mountain Press. Missoula. 1979.

19. Spellenberg, Richard. *The Audubon Society Field Guide to North American Wildflowers, Western Region.* Knopf. N.Y. 1979.

20. St. John. Harold. *Flora of Southeastern Washington.* Edwards Bros. 1963.

21. Venning, Frank D. *Wildflowers of North America.* Golden. N.Y. 1984.

22. Weber. William A. *Rocky Mountain Flora.* Colorado Univ. Boulder. 1976.

Illustrated Glossary

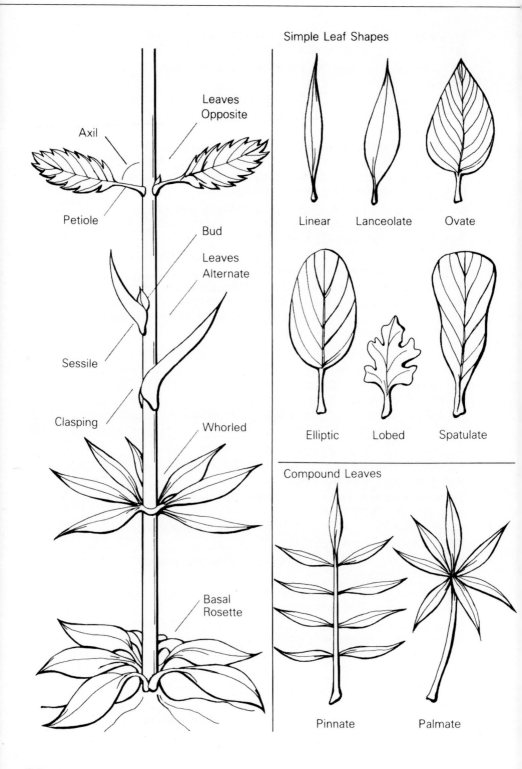

Simple Leaf Shapes

Axil

Leaves Opposite

Petiole

Bud

Leaves Alternate

Sessile

Clasping

Whorled

Basal Rosette

Linear   Lanceolate   Ovate

Elliptic   Lobed   Spatulate

Compound Leaves

Pinnate   Palmate

90

Glossary

Annual — A plant that completes its life cycle in one year.
Anther — The pollen producing appendage on the stamen.
Berry — A fleshy fruit containing seeds.
Biennial — A plant living for part or all of two years.
Bract — A leaf like scale on a flower cluster.
Bulb — A plant bud usually below ground.
Calyx — The outermost portion of a flower, the sepals collectively.
Catkin — A dense spike or raceme with many scales and small naked flowers.
Clasping — As a leaf base surrounding a stem.
Column — A group of united stamens and pistils.
Corm — A bulb-like but solid underground swelling of a stem.
Disc flower or floret — Tubular flowers at the center of a composite head.
Drupe — A fleshy fruit with a stone-encased seed.
Gland — A spot or expanded area that produces a sticky substance.
Glaucus — Fine powder coating a surface.
Head — A cluster of flowers crowding the tip of a stem.
Hybrid — Pollination of a plant by another species or variety.
Inflorescence — An arrangement of flowers on a stem.
Irregular — Nonsymmetrical in shape or orientation.
Nectar — A sweet liquid produced by flowers that attracts insects.
Node — A point on a stem where leaves or branches originate.
Ovary — Part of the pistil containing the developing seeds.
Pedicel — The supporting stem of a single flower.
Peduncle —The stalk of an inflorescence or a single flower.
Perennial — A plant that lives more than two years.
Petals — The floral leaves inside the sepals.
Petiole — The stem supporting a leaf.
Pistil — The female organ of a flower.
Pollen — Masculine cells produced by the stamens.
Raceme — An inflorescence on a single stalk composed of flowers on pedicels.
Ray flowers or florets — Strap-shaped flowers in a composite head.
Rhizome — A horizontal underground stem or rootstock.
Saprophyte — A plant that lives on dead organic matter.
Sepal — Outermost floral leaf, one segment of the calyx.
Serrate — Having short sharp teeth on the margin.
Sessile — Lacking a stem or pedicel, attached at the base.
Sheathed — Enclosing a stem at the base, clasping.
Shrub — A woody plant smaller than a tree.
Spathe — A large bract subtending or enclosing an inflorescence.
Spike — An inflorescence of sessile flowers on a single stalk.
Spur — A hollow appendage of a petal or sepal.
Stamen — The pollen producing organ of a flower.
Stigma — The end of the pistil that collects pollen.
Stolon — A horizontal stem from the base of a plant.
Style — The slender stalk of a pistil.
Succulent — Pulpy, soft and juicy.
Tendril — A slender twining extension of a leaf or stem.
Tepals — Undifferentiated sepals and petals collectively.
Umbel — A group of stems or pedicels that arise from a common point on a stalk.
Whorl — Three or more leaves or branches growing from a node or common
point.

Index

TRILLIUM, Wake Robin

Trillium ovaturm Pursh. This plant displays three exquisite petals about 2 inches long, pearly white at the peak of bloom but often turning pink or dull red with age. Three green sepals nearly as long as the petals but much narrower alternate with the petals. Six yellow anthers highlight the floral center. The solitary flower surmounts a whorl of three or more sessile leaves that are larger than the petals and nearly as broad as long. Trillium blooms early, soon after snow melt. HABITAT: Conifer forests where moist or boggy in the spring. RANGE: Southern Alberta to Colorado and west to the coast. COMMENT: We have two species of Trillium in the northern Rocky Mountain states.